The Sporting News

Presents

Mark McGwire SLUGGER!

Rob Rains

Sports Publishing Inc.

Champaign, Illinois

A portion of the proceeds from the sales of "Slugger!"
goes to the Mark McGwire Foundation for Children.

Director of Production: Susan M. McKinney
Developmental Editors: Liliana M. Lozano and Christine A. Cooper
Interior design and layout: Michelle R. Dressen
Cover design: Julie L. Denzer

Photos credits: All photos are courtesy of *The Sporting News* except: Damien
High School Yearbook, pp. 7, 8, 9; University of Southern California, pp. 11,
14; USA Baseball, pp. 15; Associated Press/Harold Jenkins, pp. 44; Front and
back cover photos courtesy of *The Sporting News.*

ISBN: 1-58261-005-3
Library of Congress Catalog Card Number: 98-86640

SPORTS PUBLISHING INC.
804 N. Neil Street, Suite 100
Champaign IL 61820
www.SportsPublishingInc.com

Printed in the United States

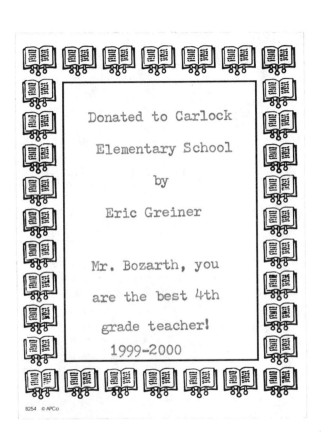

Donated to Carlock

Elementary School

by

Eric Greiner

Mr. Bozarth, you

are the best 4th

grade teacher!

1999-2000

B254 © APCo

MARK McGWIRE

plays for the St. Louis Cardinals professional baseball team. His position is first baseman. While he's really proud of where he is today, it took a lot of hard work to get there. This book tells about some of his life experiences. Maybe his experiences will help you realize that you should never give up on following your own dreams.

THE EARLY YEARS

MARK was born on October 1, 1963 in Pomona, California, to John and Ginger McGwire. He was the second oldest child of five sons. His oldest brother, Dan, went on to play professional football as a quarterback for the Seattle Seahawks, and then the Miami Dolphins. His brother, Mike, became a psychologist. Mark went on to play professional baseball as a first baseman for the Oakland Athletics, and then the St. Louis Cardinals. His brother, Bob, became a building contractor and the youngest, J.J., is a body builder and weight trainer.

IT wasn't until Mark was 8 years old that he played baseball for the first time. Some of the neighborhood kids were playing ball and invited Mark to play, too. His parents encouraged him and his four brothers to play sports. His father, John, had been an amateur boxer, and his mother, Ginger, was a swimmer in college. They always wanted their children to try their hardest, whether it was in school or on an athletic field.

MARK joined his first official Little League team, the Athletics, when he was 10 years old. He can still remember what happened the first time he came to bat; he hit his very first home run. He also remembers having one really difficult moment while playing in a Little League game. He was pitching and walked so many batters that he started crying while standing on the mound. He was having trouble seeing the batters clearly. His dad, who was also his coach, had him switch places with the short-stop. Even the view from there was fuzzy, and soon after Mark got his first pair of glasses.

MARK really liked watching baseball games. He and his family would go to California Angels games as often as they could. Even though he liked to watch the teams, he never tried to imitate any one player. Mark always wanted to play his own way. His dad later told people how he saw Mark's ability even at a young age. He said that Mark just had a sense of how to play baseball.

MARK PLAYED GOLF AND BASEBALL IN HIGH SCHOOL.

BY the time Mark was in high school, he was 6'5" and weighed more than 200 pounds. Besides playing baseball, Mark spent a lot of time learning how to play golf, and for a while, he thought he might play golf professionally. When Mark was a sophomore in high school, he won a golf tournament. He actually tied with another player and they had to play five extra playoff holes. Mark finally beat him on the fifth hole, and said the experience was very exciting.

MARK IS IN THE FIRST ROW, THIRD FROM LEFT IN THIS HIGH SCHOOL
BASKETBALL TEAM PICTURE.

EVEN though Mark enjoyed playing golf, he decided
to play other sports, too. Mark was the starting center on the
varsity basketball team at Damien High School in La Verne, California. He had fun playing basketball with his friends on the
team. He also started to play baseball again and found that he
was pretty good at it.

MARK'S SENIOR YEARBOOK PICTURE, 1981.

AS a junior in high school Mark began to think seriously about a career in baseball. Soon professional scouts and college coaches were coming from all over the country to see Mark pitch. One of the college coaches who came to see him was Marcel Lachemann, a pitching coach at the University of Southern California (USC). Though Coach Lachemann was recruiting Mark as a pitcher, he also noticed his hitting ability.

COLLEGE DAYS

THE Montreal Expos were so impressed by Mark's pitching and hitting skills that they offered him a place in their organization as soon as he graduated from high school. Mark listened to their offer, but decided going to college was more important for him. Coach Lachemann came to the McGwire house and told his family about the rich baseball tradition at USC. The McGwires were convinced that USC was the place for Mark and he was ready to begin his college career.

THE summer after Mark's freshman year in college, Assistant Coach Ron Vaughn invited Mark to play on a baseball team in Alaska, the Anchorage Glacier Pilots. Mark thought he was going to work on becoming a better pitcher, but Coach Vaughn had a different idea. He wanted to turn Mark into a first baseman. Mark says he owes a lot to Coach Vaughn because it was the first time he really took hitting seriously. He taught Mark how to stand, hold the bat, and hit the ball. Mark says Coach Vaughn probably knows more about his swing than he does.

WHEN Mark returned to school that fall, he told the head coach, Rod Dedeaux, he wanted to play first base more than pitch. He spent less time that season on his pitching, and more time improving his fielding and hitting.

Mark also spent a lot of time thinking about other things he wanted to do if his baseball career didn't work out. He was very interested in law enforcement and probably would have become a police officer if he wasn't a baseball player.

MARK continued to improve as a baseball player in college. During his junior year he set a USC record by hitting 32 home runs. The same year, Mark was named College Player of the Year by *The Sporting News* and was named first baseman for *The Sporting News* College All-America Team. Now professional scouts were looking at him as a power-hitting first baseman instead of as a pitcher.

BEFORE Mark started his professional baseball career, he was invited to play on the United States baseball team for the 1984 Olympics in Los Angeles. Before the actual Olympic Games, the team toured the United States playing exhibition games. One special moment during the tour was when Mark got to meet Hall of Famer Reggie Jackson at one of the games. During that game Mark hit a home run estimated at 450 feet. Many of Mark's Olympic teammates also went on to become successful major league baseball players.

(MARK IS THIRD FROM LEFT IN THIS PHOTO.)

THE MINOR LEAGUES

MARK began playing in the minor leagues for the Oakland Athletics (A's) for their Class A California League team. He was only able to play in 16 games before the season ended, but he did hit his first professional home run.

DURING the following season, the coaches wanted Mark to try playing third base. This was a difficult change for Mark. He soon developed a reputation as a hot head, a player who quickly lost his temper. He would throw bats around whenever a call didn't go his way. One night Mark was watching another player lose his temper and he realized how silly he must look. This convinced him that he needed to change the way he was acting.

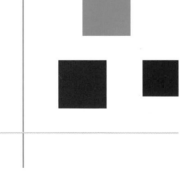

DURING the 1986 season, Mark was promoted to Oakland's Class AA Huntsville, Alabama team. He continued to improve and was promoted again to the A's top farm club, Tacoma, Washington in the Class AAA Pacific Coast League. Mark played there for two months, hitting 13 home runs and driving in 59 runs. It was then that the A's decided he was ready for the next level. On August 20, 1986, Mark found out he was going to play in the major leagues for the Oakland A's.

THE OAKLAND A'S

FOR Mark, starting in the major leagues wasn't an instant success. He went hitless in his first two games, but collected his first major league single on August 24, 1986.

The very next day Mark hit his first career home run, measured at 450 feet, at Tiger Stadium in Detroit.

Mark was still trying to adjust to his third base position. He ended up making so many errors that he was moved back to his natural spot at first base.

AT spring training for the following season, Mark was hoping to play well enough to stay in the majors and not have to return to the minors. He was in competition for the first base position with another rookie player. Manager Tony La Russa wasn't sure which player to choose, so he kept both of them on the roster. While neither player got off to a great start, Manager La Russa gave Mark

most of the playing time. He soon named Mark as the full-time first baseman. It was a good boost for his confidence to have someone believe in his playing ability. Around this time Mark also found out that his wife was pregnant with their first child. All the confidence he was gaining helped Mark to improve his game. He had be-came the first rookie in history to hit 30 home runs before the All-Star break.

NEAR the end of the 1987 season, Mark had broken the team record of 47 home runs that was held by Reggie Jackson. Going into the last game of the year, he only needed one more home run to reach 50. The morning of the game Mark's then-wife called to tell him she was about to have their baby. He flew back home just in time to see his son, Matthew, being born. Mark might have missed the chance to become the first rookie in history to hit 50 home runs, but to him, Matthew was his 50th home run. The combination of his son's birth and being named the American League Rookie of the Year, made it an incredible season for Mark.

MARK realized that after such a good season, people were going to expect even more of him. The A's were building a great team with players such as Jose Canseco (at left, with Mark), Dennis Eckersley, Carney Lansford, Dave Stewart, and Bob Welch. Mark said it was an amazing experience to play on such a talented team. They worked very hard and won the American League West title in 1988. Even though they didn't win the World Series, they were proud of their accomplishments.

THE 1988 American League Championship was the first of three straight division titles for Oakland. By the third time the A's had reached their goal, the team was so used to winning that they took their success for granted. It bothered Mark that his teammates just expected to win, and he was worried that everyone had forgotten about all of their hard work and practice. Mark feels everyone should always remember to be grateful and appreciate the special moments in their lives.

WHILE the team was successful, Mark knew he wasn't happy, and it was affecting his game. He needed time to talk to someone and work through his problems. He went to a counselor who helped Mark find out what was important in his life again. Sometimes you might face a big problem, too. It's always okay for you to talk to someone you trust about what is troubling you.

AS Mark began to feel better about himself, he also wanted to improve on his baseball skills. He began weightlifting and tried new eye exercises to help improve his eyesight. Soon Mark's performance began to improve.

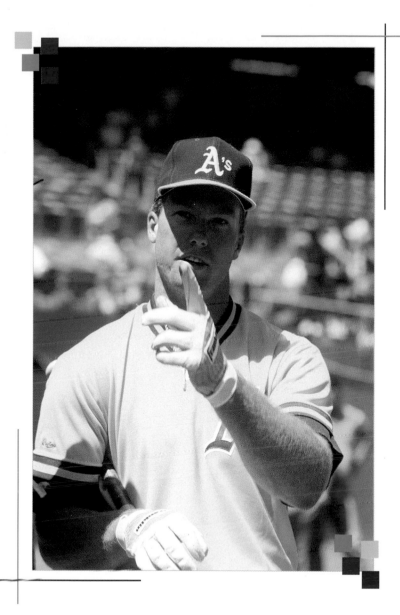

ONE of the hardest lessons Mark learned in his life is that his attitude affected how well he played baseball. Mark felt he needed a good attitude, along with physical strength, to play well. Sometimes the toughest experiences in life are the ones that teach you the most.

MARK then suffered several seasons of injuries, and he began to question his future in baseball. But with the support of his family and his friends, Mark decided to keep playing. He was still injured, but he made up his mind to get back in the game sooner than everyone expected. After much hard work, Mark felt healthy, strong and ready to play as he headed back onto the field for the 1996 season.

BY the end of June, 1996, Mark had hit 25 home runs. He hit 13 more in July, including a 488-foot shot, the longest home run ever hit in Toronto's Skydome. By September 7, his number of home runs climbed to 48. Mark finally reached his 50th home run on September 14 in Cleveland. All Mark could think about as he

rounded the bases was how he had always promised his son, Matt, that he could have his 50th home run baseball. Mark was able to keep his promise to Matt when he got the ball back from the fan who caught it. Mark finished the 1996 season with a total of 52 homers.

THE ST. LOUIS CARDINALS

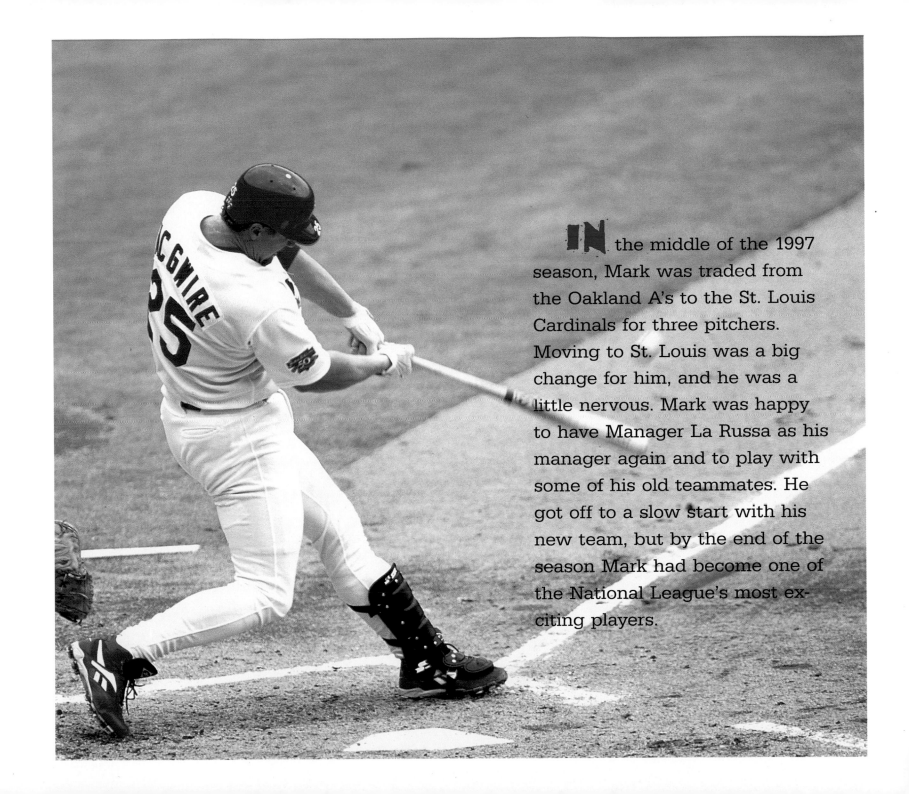

IN the middle of the 1997 season, Mark was traded from the Oakland A's to the St. Louis Cardinals for three pitchers. Moving to St. Louis was a big change for him, and he was a little nervous. Mark was happy to have Manager La Russa as his manager again and to play with some of his old teammates. He got off to a slow start with his new team, but by the end of the season Mark had become one of the National League's most exciting players.

MARK soon felt comfortable in St. Louis. After finishing the last half of the season, he decided he wanted to stay with the Cardinals. Mark appreciated the way the front office and the fans treated him. It didn't take him long to fall in love with the Cardinals and the city of St. Louis. Mark says he feels like he's floating every time he plays in Busch Stadium. When Mark called his son, Matt, to tell him that he was going to sign with St. Louis, Matt said, "All right!" It was very important to Mark that his son was happy.

MARK said it was amazing as he went up to bat the night after he signed his contract with the Cardinals. Everyone was on their feet and cheering, and Mark knew he was home. All of the fans' energy helped him hit the longest home run in Busch Stadium at that time, 517 feet. By the end of the 1997 season, Mark was also named Sportsman of the Year by *The Sporting News*. He also became the first player in history to hit 20 or more home runs for two different teams in the same season.

AFTeR that, it only got better for Mark. He started the 1998 season by becoming the first Cardinal ever to hit a grand slam on opening day. Two weeks later, with his son Matt as the Cardinals' bat boy, (shown at right) Mark slugged three home runs in a game at Busch Stadium.

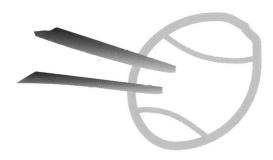

MARK enjoyed some special moments, like when Manager La Russa introduced him to Cardinal Hall of Famer, Stan Musial. Mark says he was honored to meet Mr. Musial and feels that players need to appreciate what the former stars went through to help make baseball as exciting as it is today.

MARK is often compared to another baseball legend, Babe Ruth. He is the only player besides The Bambino to hit 50 or more home runs in back-to-back seasons. Mark hits home runs almost as often as Ruth did while he was playing baseball.

Although it has never been Mark's goal, he could break Roger Maris' major league record of 61 home runs in a single season.

MARK knows how fortunate he is to be a professional baseball player. Even when times got tough, he never gave less than his best. It takes a lot of hard work, patience, and believing in yourself to reach your goals in life. By pursuing his own talents, Mark was able to fulfill his own dreams. Wherever your dreams may lead you, always remember,

THE SKY IS THE LIMIT!

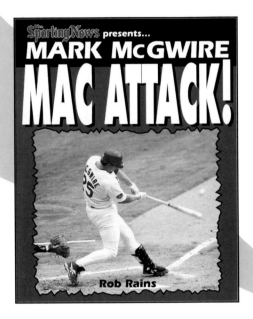

presents

Mark McGwire: Mac Attack!

Mark McGwire: Mac Attack! is geared toward children ages 12-15. It is a biography of the baseball superstar who has learned many lessons during his career and childhood. *Mark McGwire: Mac Attack!* is a softcover book and includes 40+ photos.

AVAILABLE NOW

To order call
1-800-327-5557

It's a Home Run!

• Baseball • Basketball • Football • Hockey

The Teams... The Stats... The Strategies... Every week, in season & out.
Trades, Drafts and Deals. Revealing insights and commentary.

See a Different Game

SAVE 74%
Special New Subscriber Offer

Get 30 issues of *The Sporting News* for just 75¢ each
(74% off the newsstand price).

Call Toll-Free 1-800-950-1341

5MGB6